To: Caleb

Thank you for your support

9live's
"Finding a Way Out"

by

Andrew Ross

Copyright © 2012 Andrew Ross
All rights reserved.

ISBN: 1478336854
ISBN-13: 9781478336853

"All Scripture quotations taken from THE HOLY BIBLE, NEW INTERNATIONAL VERSION®, NIV® Copyright © 1973, 1978, 1984, 2011 by Biblica, Inc.™

Dedication

First I give praise and honor to my Lord and Savior Jesus Christ for allowing the Holy Spirit to use me to fill the pages of this book with my life journey.

These pages are dedicated to my family—my mother, my sister, my brother, and my daughter—for their unconditional love and support of me. To my father, may he rest in peace for his lessons of tough love and life; they have shaped me into the man I am today.

To the young brothers and sisters who have lost their lives during the struggle for self-love and acceptance, as well as those who remain in the struggle.

Hold on, it gets better.

Because God is...

Table of contents

Dedication		iii
Introduction		vii
Chapter 1	Finding Your Way out of Abuse: "I Am Afraid of Changing Because I Built My Life around You"	1
Chapter 2	Finding Your Way out of Codependency: The Need to Be Needed	13
Chapter 3	Finding Your Way out of Darkness: God, Me, and the Devil	27
Chapter 4	Finding Your Way out of Isolation: A Day in the Life of a Caveman	43
Chapter 5	Finding Your Way out of Pain: Addicted to Pain	57
Chapter 6	Finding Your Way out of Self-Doubt: You Are Worth More than You Think	71
Chapter 7	Finding Your Way toward Balance Temperament: A Diamond in the Rough	83
Chapter 8	Finding Your Way toward Purpose: A Mission to Live on Purpose	93

Introduction

I know how to abase and I know how to abound. Everywhere and in all things I have learned both to be full and to be hungry, both to abound and to suffer need.

I can do all things through Christ who strengthens me.

—Philippians 4:12–13

For fifteen years, I searched for my purpose. I used alcohol and drugs to fill what seemed to be a never-ending void in my life. Then I came to discover that this void I chased could only be filled by the grace and love of God.

I had become so hopeless at the lowest point of my life that I can recall wanting to ingest drugs and inflict pain upon myself to help fill the emptiness.

I even put a razor blade in my nose to attempt to cut away the thoughts the enemy had placed in my head. The self-inflected injury resulted in hours of severe bleeding. Despite the trauma to my body, I would go on to abuse drugs for years in my pointless and selfish attempt to fill my internal emptiness.

I have been blessed to make it out of my life-threatening situations, as well as my mental and emotional hell, but the nature of finding my way out also seeks to pull me back in on a daily basis.

I struggle daily with the demons of my past and the call of Christ upon my life. The struggle has taught me that we never completely rid ourselves of our challenges; we learn to control our weaknesses as we grow and develop our strengths.

9live's "Finding a Way Out"

While I was experiencing what I refer to as my personal hell, I always felt a sense of spiritual covering from God—a still voice saying, "There is a better way, and I will cover you always."

My inability to cope with personal issues was compounded by the fact that I had no positive social outlets as a young boy, and my home environment was restrictive and abusive. My struggles in school were both social and academic, which further affected the void of hopelessness I could not escape.

Rather than attend class, I chose to sell drugs and fight to prove my worth and value. When I decided upon this path, I was not the best fighter. In fact, I could not fight at all. During the progression of my fifteen-year battle, I became very good at fighting, selling drugs, and masking my feelings of emptiness.

By the time I was in eighth grade, my self-esteem was shot, despite the fact that I was a very handsome young man. I could not get past doubting my value and self-worth. By this time in my life, I was so broken I was unable to accept the smallest attempt of another person to express feelings of concern or love for me. These feelings were unable to penetrate my deep-rooted pain that I could not overcome.

I would hope to die so I could be taken out of my misery. I recall taking a syringe, filling it with ice-cold water, and shooting the water into a vein in my arm. I hoped it would freeze my heart, my heart would stop beating, and the pain would end, because I would have ended my life.

By God's grace, however, had a different plan for me to use my pain to help others who may have the same feelings of hopelessness and despair in their lives.

The unbeliever might call me lucky because my ice-water attempt did not work. However, as a born-again Christian, I consider myself blessed. The unmerited grace of God covered me when the enemy clearly wanted to end my life, making countless attempts over the course of my fifteen-year hellish experience. This can only be understood by being in a relationship to Christ.

I remember chasing feelings, people, places, and things in an attempt to avoid myself. I searched not just in substance and violence. I also looked for God, thinking to myself, *Yeah! God is the answer to my problems.* I sought God in many denominations. At one point in my life, I studied the satanic bible and worshipped the devil. I worshiped the devil as my god for many years and continued to question why I did not see change happening in the wounded areas of my life.

I was so enmeshed in darkness that I had experiences in which I tapped into the spirit realm and saw evil spirits. I literally climbed through the walls of my apartment to chase the spirits out.

My life shifted toward the light of Christ nine years ago, when I gave my life over to Jesus Christ. I attended a Sunday service at Christian Cultural Center in Brooklyn, New York, where A. R.

9live's "Finding a Way Out"

Bernard is the founder and head pastor. On that fateful Sunday morning, the Holy Spirit used Pastor Bernard to bring the light of Christ into my heart and heal places that no drug or self-inflected pain could heal during my fifteen-year search. It was on that Sunday that the fifteen years of hell came to a complete stop, and a new purpose and drive replaced my pain.

The tests of my life are my testimony. They are what I had to experience so God could mold me into what he needed me to be for the kingdom and for his glory. It has been the full grace of God that has allowed me to overcome poverty, homelessness, and gang involvement, as well as being a high-school dropout and a consumer and distributor of drugs.

I am now a three-time graduate, having received my bachelor's degree in human services, an MPA in emergency disaster management, and an MBA in general management. Additionally, I am board certified as a personal fitness trainer by the National Academy for Sports Medicine.

The challenges of poor self-love and self-acceptance are very common in our society. They are feelings that don't discriminate by age, gender, or socioeconomic status. These issues affect most people. It is the capacity to grow, despite having to manage these issues that can create life-changing and world-changing men and women of God.

In the following chapters, we will begin to explore some of the tools I used and still use to support the lasting changes I have made in my life.

Seeking to hear daily the voice of the Lord, practicing diligence and discipline, taking responsibility, and maintaining balance are some of the strategies I used to help me find my way out.

We will continue to unpack the hell that I personally experienced while we explore developing skills to help you, the reader, create lasting change in your own life.

We all have a purpose, as we have been fearfully and wonderfully made by the hands of God. I challenge you to pay close attention to my life story, my experiences, and the solutions I will share in helping you create a life for yourself that is balanced and free of the vices that can keep us all in bondage in one way or another.

At the end of each chapter, I will give you a turning point and a sparkplug. The turning points should be used to help you find the strength, often needed to create an opportunity in your life to find a way out of whatever it is you may need freedom from. The sparkplugs will be a series of reflective questions. You should be very thoughtful in answering, as the responses to the questions, in addition to the motivation of the turning point, will be the tools needed to help you find your way out.

Let's begin our journey by putting God before us and asking that he open our hearts and our minds to be renewed.

Chapter 1

Finding Your Way out of Abuse:

"I Am Afraid of Changing Because I Built My Life around You."

I will say of the Lord, He is my refuge and my fortress; My God, in Him I will trust, surely He shall deliver you from the snare of the fowler and from the perilous pestilence. He shall cover you with His feathers, and under his wings you shall take refuge.

—Psalm 91:2–4

When I was growing up, my mother was a stay-at-home mom. She made sure our home ran like a well-oiled machine. She completed the daily tasks of cooking, doing laundry, and taking my siblings and me to and from school with pride each and every day.

These tasks were expected of her. My dad was raised with real Southern values, and he believed a woman's job was to care for and raise her family. Having a career or a formal education would have never been expected of my mother. Neither my father nor my mother considered it. He was the breadwinner, the provider, and the alpha male. He paid all the bills on time and kept a roof over our heads.

It sounds very ideal, the loving husband going out making a living to provide for his family, coupled with the stay-at-home wife who takes pride in her clean home, raising her three children, and loving her husband. The reality was that my home environment was far from ideal.

Abuse, isolation, and misdirected or unresolved anger, all expressed by my dad, were the seeds planted in my home. These seeds gave root to low self-esteem, no self-worth, and fear. These seeds were rooted in all of my family members and would manifest in all of us in different ways over the course of our lives.

9live's "Finding a Way Out"

The physical and mental abuse my mother experienced from my dad caused her to literally go crazy. Behavior she was being accused of in the home became behavior she began to perform, simply because she had been conditioned to believe she was in fact performing that very behavior.

When you live in an abusive environment, you make every effort to prevent the cycle from starting again. My mother would keep things from my father, so as to not anger him. Sometimes this tactic would work, and other times it would not.

After years of abuse, I learned that you can't please an abuser, and you just pray that tonight won't be the night you get the air knocked out of your lungs.

My dad's sense of family was distorted. He believed we did not need anyone but us, the people who lived within the four walls of my home. At night he would board the backdoor with huge pieces of wood, and he would never allow us to open up the curtains.

We were made to live a very isolated life; friends, family, and neighbors were seldom allowed to come over. Events like holidays or birthday get-togethers were events that I never experienced as a child.

When my dad would come in from work, his daily routine was to be served dinner by my mom, pour himself a shot of scotch, and light up a cigarette. My guess is that he needed to maintain as much of a controlled, ritual-like existence to help calm the rage that smoldered inside of him.

The fear of his abusive episodes prevented us from living a life free of fear. In fact, fear is all we knew. I can recall having said something to my dad that triggered him so badly that I was beaten within inches of my life. He would hit me with such force his glasses would fall off of his face. In those moments, I would lovingly assist him in looking for them, despite the fact that the moment before he was beating me as if I were a grown man.

My attempt to love my dad in those moments only resulted in his anger increasing and him resuming the beating. To escape the hitting from hands at least two sizes larger than an average man's hands, I would run and hide in the closet for an opportunity to catch my breath. But those moments were short lived because he would find me and hit me harder.

After the hitting stopped for the night, I would think, *Why? Why does he do this to us, to me, to her?* I recall saying to myself, "I guess he beats us and hurts us because, when he looks at me, he sees himself." Hurting us was his way of dealing with his own failures and shortcomings.

My dad ran away from his birth home at the age of fifteen. While making a life for himself, he connected with some very shady characters, the likes of which got my dad involved in stealing, hustling, and other similar crimes.

My dad could have written his own book about the things he had experienced. What caused him to leave home and go out into the world to fight for his survival I will never know. However, I do know his values were imposed on our family and created most, if not all, of the demons I have spent the past fifteen years running away from. Abuse can be so embedded in the psyche of a person that even when the abuse stops, the abused may act out and behave as if the abuse were still going on.

My dad passed away in 2005, and the seeds planted within the members of my family will take years to be uprooted. The seeds manifested themselves in the form of substance abuse, mental illness, poor self-worth, and weak self-value.

The cycle of abuse experienced in my family went on from my ninth birthday until I developed enough courage to leave my parents' home at the age of seventeen.

While I remained in the home, the abuse my family and I experienced at the hands of my father could be defined as a classic abusive dynamic.

> *Tension build up:* The tension would increase, based on something that was said or done.
>
> *Abusive episode:* The point in the cycle in which the abuse is at its most intense.
>
> *Reconciliation:* The abuser makes every effort to be loving and affectionate toward the abused to regain trust and loyalty.
>
> *Calm:* This is the point in the cycle in which the abused can sense that the active abuse will soon happen.

The predictable stages of abuse are a mirrored truth of what we experienced in my home. The affectionate and loving times in the cycle were when I was able to learn from my father good qualities and good disciplines and to make some sense out of why he needed to love us in the hurtful way he did.

I was able to maintain hope that my dad was capable of loving us without pain and hurt. It was at this stage that I would develop a set of core values that would be so deeply rooted that I know they were divinely branded into my spirit by God himself.

The abuse I experienced in the home was the first piece of the puzzle of my life, the trauma that I had to live through to be what God needed me to become. I believe that in our human existence, we must be faced with pain, hurt, and disappointment to a certain degree to allow us to go deeper into our understanding and dependency upon God. These situations, if allowed, can be used as motivators, as opportunities to build in us strength while helping to develop a Christlike character in us.

The difference between someone who remains in an abusive situation and someone who gets out of the situation is belief in self. It is the belief that you are worth being loved, that you are worth having a good life, and that God loves you and wants the best for you in this life, even if that abuse is coming from a parent.

The challenge for many of us is not having a role model to help develop that sense of self-love that would never allow you to be abused, or to abuse yourself.

Not having that in my life, I had to develop this skill with the help of the Holy Spirit. Learning to become still enough, so you can clearly hear yourself speak words of strength over your life, is a vital step in this change. It is important to speak words of strength, life, and empowerment over yourself even when no one else will.

TURNING POINT

Learning how to develop the skill to be good to yourself is a lifetime commitment. Choosing to care for yourself first can and will be a challenge, as many of us are not used to functioning this way. We often feel focusing on self is selfish. However, this notion is far from the truth. Finding real happiness in this life starts and stops with you.

I'm not giving you permission to forget about everyone else and disengage from the world just because you are focusing on yourself. Instead, it is an attempt to have men and women change their way of thinking and learn how to treat themselves better. If you are in an abusive relationship, take the steps you need to address the issue. If you are drinking and drugging every day, love yourself enough to get help. If you smoke a pack of cigarettes per day, it's never too late to stop.

SPARKPLUGS

Consider the following questions, and think of your responses before actually writing down your answers. Be as honest with yourself as you can. Answering the questions won't be the end. I am charging you to review your progress weekly, and if there are tasks you need to get done, do them. I would lastly recommend that you keep a journal of your progress.

Your thought process and responses to the list of questions will start you on your journey of self-love, acceptance, and change.

- *Are you spending time with God daily?*

- *What is the abuse you want to be released from?*

- *What are the things you are currently doing to invest in yourself?*

- *What are three things you like about yourself?*

- *What steps have you taken or will you take in the next thirty days to create the release you are seeking?*

Notes:

Andrew Ross

Chapter 2

Finding Your Way out of Codependency:

The Need to Be Needed

You shall have no other gods before me.

—Exodus 20:3

Andrew Ross

We were not created to be alone. We all strive to be needed. However, there are some who are extreme in their need to be needed. This group of people will hurt themselves and others as a means of punishment to attract the attention of another, gaining love by any means necessary.

When I was about sixteen years old, I was very afraid to walk from school to the store and then home. I would take shortcuts to avoid the neighborhood bullies. Sharing with my parents that I was being bullied was not an option. My dad's style of parenting eventually created such low self-esteem in us that we all grew up wanting to be needed by everyone we met, despite the dangers these relationships would place us in.

I eventually grew out of the fear of going to the store and began working at a local supermarket, packing grocery bags for customers and earning twenty-five cents to a dollar per customer. I wanted to earn my own money to buy sneakers and whatever the in-style gear was at that time. It was yet another attempt to be accepted.

I recall making enough money at one point to buy a pair of leather Playboy shoes, with the bunny on the side, and a pair of blue leather pants; I just knew I had it going on.

Monday through Sunday I would go to the supermarket to pack bags, provided my dad was in the mood to allow me to go.

9live's "Finding a Way Out"

There were times when he would keep us locked in the house as a form of punishment.

The bullies who gave me problems in school also began to harass me at my job. They would wait outside the store for me so they could take the money I had earned.

I had to develop a strategy of getting out of the store without them seeing me and taking my money. I learned the streets and alleyways from the store to my home very well by the time I stopped packing bags. These plans to avoid the bullies on a daily basis took a large amount of time, and I recall feeling exhausted because I literally had no outlet. I was getting bullied at school and in my community and getting abused at home.

Having nowhere to turn, I met this young lady who did not live too far from my home. She turned out to be the first girl I had sex with and also the first to give me a sexually transmitted disease. After the sexual encounter, I got up several days later to discover I had an off-white discharge coming from my penis, and I felt a burning sensation, which I never want to feel again. Yes, I got burned. Because of my home life, I was afraid to tell my parents, so I cut school and went to a clinic in the Bronx. It was there that I had my first experience with the largest syringe I had ever seen. I had to get a one-time shoot in my buttocks to cure the discharge and burning. My home life caused me to seek sex and relationships with women as another attempt to escape the void of love, affection, and connection.

At the age of fifteen, I thought I had actually found love when I met a young Latina woman while hanging out at McDonald's.

We started talking and exchanged phone numbers, and we were inseparable from that time on. We did everything together for the next year of my life, including getting high together. It was this relationship that introduced me to smoking marijuana. I found in her the love and affection I did not get from home. In my mind, we would spend the rest of our lives together. But I discovered she did not feel the same. Just as we approached our first-year anniversary, I found the love of my life in the basement of her home making out with another man.

The hurt of this betrayal created such a feeling of rejection in my spirit that I spent the next twenty years trying to get past this pain.

Over the next twenty years, I slept with countless women. I went into relationships knowing I did not care for the women and did not want long-term relationships. I knowingly would abuse and misuse them. I am guilty of having hurt women based on my inability to love and be loved the way relationships and love were divinely intended.

To numb my feelings of coping with the abuse in every area of my life, I began to use having sex with random women, smoking weed, and drinking to dull the feelings I was experiencing. The feelings I experienced from the drugs made me feel at peace, or at least that is what I thought after the first time I got high. The need to be needed and accepted began to pull me into the wrong crowd of people. I was so desperate to feel needed that I was blinded to the character of the people I was around.

I was tricked into feeling that this group of guys I connected with had my best interests at heart. I trusted them to prepare the drugs we would take without considering that they wanted to keep me high and out of sorts. It was here that I learned the hard way that people who hurt want to hurt people.

One time we were hanging out, getting high, and one of the guys pulled out of his pocket two red-topped capsules that had powered rock inside.

When I asked what it was, the guy responded, "It will make you feel like Superman." Trusting the crew, I smoked this substance along with everyone else. I found out later that night that the substance was cocaine. They cheered and supported me as I crossed over into another level of getting high, the same as you would be congratulated for graduating from college. I thought, *This group of guys is my new family.* I had finally found the acceptance I had been searching for.

Feeling accepted and needed was the best feeling ever, even if the group accepting me was made up of crack-cocaine-smoking, going-nowhere-fast losers. I didn't care because they didn't beat me up, and they wanted to hang out with me whether I had money or not.

The connection was amazing, and the drugs gave me courage to approach the ladies, but without the drugs, I was very shy. The alcohol made me feel like I could stand up to the biggest, baddest dude on the block, and the cocaine numbed me in the event I got my butt whipped for running my mouth.

The acceptance I found on the street with this group of guys filled the void I had in my home life. My dad terrified the entire family to the point that we all wanted to leave, but we depended upon him for life-sustaining provisions: food, money, and shelter. We depended upon him to determine the feelings we would have on any given day. If he was happy, we were all happy, but if he was sad, we were all sad. If he was angry, either my mother or I got beaten, and my siblings suffered emotionally.

The control in my home was so engrained in all of us that my dad even controlled the way we cared for our pets. We had two rabbits and a dog. I can't recall ever walking the dog; he stayed caged on the back patio for years. We never cleaned the cage the rabbits lived in. If we were told to tend to the animals, which seldom happened, we did. If we weren't told to tend to them, we didn't. Even the animals weren't shown love and affection to make them feel wanted and loved.

All living things need to be needed, man and animal alike. However, if we become so focused upon filling that need that we lose sight of self and most importantly lose sight of God, then the relationship, the connection we are so desperate to make, will be doomed to fail. The sex, drugs, and poor decision making came from not having any other means of understanding that I needed to love myself.

I had to get to a place in my personal growth in which I understood who I was. The need I had to be needed had to come from a place of divine peace rather than a place of self-centeredness and immediate gratification. I discovered that I could only do this through having a relationship with Jesus Christ.

In developing my relationship with Christ and learning to need him and depend on him, all the other dependencies were no longer needed. The drugs, the empty and meaningless sex with women, and the abuse of alcohol had to leave my life. Walking with Christ has become the center of my existence.

These built-up dependencies prevent us from taking inventory of ourselves—our past, our present, and our future selves. We use these vices to mask the truth of where we are, the pain we feel, and the changes we need to make to become the well-balanced, self-loving, and self-accepting men and women in Christ we have been created to be.

I have always thought the biggest challenge in life was to evaluate yourself, but I was wrong. The biggest challenge in life is allowing yourself to be loved. Allowing yourself to be loved is more challenging because, deep down inside, we convince ourselves we are not worthy of being loved. We all go around pretending to love one another, not having done the work of first loving ourselves.

TURNING POINT

Learning to love yourself comes from knowing who your heavenly Father is, knowing that you were chosen to live in this time, on this planet, with a divine purpose in the mind of God. Just knowing that should be enough to get the wheels of change moving in your head.

The relationships we develop all satisfy a need in our lives in some way. We develop connections with people for a reason, a season, or a lifetime. The people we meet are meant to grow us to the next level and prepare us for the next level, and many will leave our lives before we arrive at our next level. We get stuck on the idea of needing people because we allow the spirit of fear to make us believe we need the abusive partner. We need the group

of friends because no one else will accept us, or we feel like we're not good enough to venture past the six-block radius of our community. We even engage in sexual relationships very prematurely because we want to be connected.

The most lasting, most effective, and most productive way to connect with others is by first spending time in the presence of God and second by spending time alone with yourself. Spending time alone with yourself will allow you to discover what makes you happy, mad, or sad. Time alone will help you develop goals for your life, both long term and short term. It also allows you to understand your strengths and weaknesses and develop skills to minimize your weaknesses as you build upon your strengths. All of these are key to developing relationships that are balanced and healthy.

SPARKPLUGS

Consider the following questions and think of your responses before actually writing down your answers. Be as honest with yourself as you can. Answering the questions won't be the end. I am charging you to review your progress weekly, and if there are tasks you need to get done, do them. I would lastly recommend that you keep a journal of your progress.

Your thought process and responses to the list of questions will start you on your journey of self-love, acceptance, and change.

❖ *Are you spending time in the presence of God daily?*

❖ *What is your purpose?*

❖ *What are your strengths?*

❖ *What are your weaknesses?*

❖ *What relationships are you currently in that are unhealthy?*

Notes:

Andrew Ross

Chapter 3

Finding Your Way out of Darkness:

God, Me, and the Devil

And the devil, taking him up into a high mountain, showed him all the kingdoms of the world in a moment of time. And the devil said unto him, all this power will I give thee, and the glory of them: for that is delivered unto me; and to whomsoever I will, give it. If you therefore will worship me, all shall be given to you.

—**Luke 4:5–7**

Attending church in my childhood was something that did not happen too often. My dad did acknowledge that there was a God, but he never really helped us make the connection with the God he spoke of and how we should include him in our lives. He would make comments like, "God is good," and I would say to myself, *If there really is a God, why do we wonder if we will have a hot meal on the table tonight? If there is a God, why does he allow my father to hurt us the way he does?* I questioned the existence of God.

In my attempt to quiet my demons, I ventured into several denominations to see if I could find the relief I was searching for. I experimented with the Catholic, Baptist, and Islamic religions. During this experimental phase, I continued to question the reality of God and his value in my life and the lives of others in the world because bad things always happened to good people. If God was real, he would not allow good people like me to get hurt, to feel so much pain, and not help us.

After several unsuccessful attempts at connecting with an authority higher than myself, I came upon Satanism. For years I lived under the full direction of the devil. This connection falsely allowed me to believe that if the people who bullied and persecuted me knew I worshiped the devil, they would fear me and leave me alone.

9live's "Finding a Way Out"

During this time of complete darkness in my life, I was still drinking and using drugs, which the enemy used to his advantage to further pull me into his deception and lies.

At one time, I had been up all night drinking and reading the satanic bible when I began to see spirits, dark shadows, and figures moving throughout my apartment. During this same episode, I also saw newborn babies who looked as if they had been burned alive. I could see the black char on their bodies and smell the stench of burnt flesh. I would also feel spirits pass by me and through my body.

As gross and horrific as this sounds, I was not afraid because I felt that I had found a connection. I was able to connect with these spirits of the dark, and I felt they would protect me from the other things that were happening to me in this realm. I had not made the connection that evil is evil. What we struggle with in this life, or in this realm, first exists in the spiritual realm. My demons of fear, low self-esteem, and drugs were all behaviors and feelings that were being used by the devil to kill me.

During this time, I had the horrible experience of having a very good friend get killed in the apartment above me. Bubbles and I had been friends for a number of years, and due to a silly misunderstanding, we had fallen out and had stopped speaking. On the day Bubbles was killed, I was in my apartment getting high with another friend when we heard a very loud noise. We heard the noise but assumed Bubbles was moving furniture around. I did not think to see what might be going on because I was getting high and because Bubbles and I had fallen out a few days prior.

Just about a half hour later, I decided to leave my apartment and go to the front of the building. It was then that I discovered that the loud noise we had heard just thirty minutes earlier was my good friend falling down the stairs to his death. When I left my apartment, I discovered the dead, lifeless body of my good friend at the bottom of the stairs. In an attempt to get help, he crawled from his apartment and had fallen down the stairs. Some young kids had gotten into his apartment, robbed him, and cut his throat, killing him.

After the murder of Bubbles, I went deeper into the worship of Satan. It was almost as if the enemy was forcing me into a state of complete isolation and torment. I was so heavily involved in my relationship with the devil that my physical appearance changed as well. I was physically drawn in, my skin color had changed, and I had begun to resemble that of a zombie. When I did go outside, the people who once bullied me would cross the street to get away from me. Initially, I thought this was good. My new means of coping was getting me the result that I longed for, which was not to be bullied.

What I would later learn was that my false sense of accomplishment in keeping the bullies away enabled me to make a tangible connection with Satan that would hurt me far worse than the bullying did. The enemy led me to believe I could consume volumes of drugs that, under normal circumstances, would have killed the person ingesting them.

I was drinking and snorting so much cocaine that I would hemorrhage, and clots of blood the size of golf balls would come out of my nose. My mother would come over every now and again to visit me as I was going through this hell, and she would see my bed sheets saturated with blood. I can hear her crying, even now, at the horrifying amount of blood that was all over my apartment.

One of the statements I would recite on a daily basis from the satanic bible was, "Your soul will belong to the devil." After saying the prayer, it was almost as if I could unlock the doorway to the spirit world, because I would begin to feel spirits moving though my apartment and through my body almost at will. Voices would tell me to take sharp objects and pierce my nose. I was convinced that harming myself would make me stop using drugs. Between the self-inflicted injuries and the trauma caused by using the drugs, blood was the décor of my apartment. I was always bleeding.

Spiritual warfare is very real and should not be taken lightly. Satan would tell me to take a sharp object to open my flesh in an attempt to get the spirits out of my body. During this time, the devil was trying to take my life. I made several attempts at committing suicide. I put a gun to my head, but the bullet got stuck in the gun's chamber. I shot cold water in my veins in an attempt to stop my heart, but my arm just got cold. I also attempted to hang myself, but my foot got caught in the curtain at the window, so instead of hanging myself I tripped. I could have died as a result of having lost excessive amounts of blood from the drugs and other self-infected injuries. But God...

In April of 1990, at the height of my worshipping the devil, I experienced even more tragedy. I was attacked on the streets of the Bronx and was left for dead. A member of a rival gang attacked me over a territory beef that had taken place two months prior to this particular confrontation. He caught me in the Bronx and beat me with a lead pipe. Most of the injuries I sustained were to my head. The damage he had done caused a crack in my skull and blood clots to form on my brain.

When I was found, I was rushed to the hospital and was not given a good prognosis in terms of living to recover from the injuries. My parents were told that I needed to be operated on within ten minutes of me having arrived at the hospital, or I would die. I underwent the surgery, and the surgeon was able to remove the blood clots from my brain, but my chances of getting through the night were still very slim. The priest was called to my bedside, and I lay in a coma for two days. Everyone thought this was my end. But God…

After having recovered a bit, I decided the Bronx was not where I needed to be. I had lived in that demon-consumed apartment for one year. Six months after the operation, I decided to move back to Queens. I thought the worst was behind me. Moving out of the Bronx was my way out.

I could not have been more wrong. Soon after I got back to Queens, I bumped into another person with whom I had problems. This time, instead of beating me, the person got one good punch in and dislocated my cheekbone, broke my jaw, dislocated my nose, and gave me two black eyes.

As my face, my body, and my ego healed, I decided Satan was not helping me; he was trying to kill me. However, despite Satan's attempts, the God who created the heavens and the earth had his hand in and upon my life. God would not allow the devil to kill me.

In 1996, just about eleven years after I had picked up the satanic bible, I put it down and picked up the New International Version of the Bible (NIV). I began reading in yet another attempt to find some relief, direction, and safety. I wanted to understand the goodness of God, but I was still being plagued by thoughts of evil.

In that same year, I opened my heart up to the Lord Jesus Christ. I sat still long enough to hear a very quiet voice say, "Your life was not given to you that you might suffer this way. I sent my Son to die on the cross for your sins, that you might have life and have it abundantly." I heard these words from the Lord.

Despite the hell I lived in for many years, I did learn a very valuable lesson by having sought the devil as a means of producing happiness in my life. I learned to believe, with everything that I am, that the devil is a liar, and if you pray and seek instruction from a lower authority, the consequences of that choice will be to settle for less and to expect the worst to manifest in your life.

Deciding to honor, glorify, and seek the high power of God will only manifest goodness and the gifts of the Holy Spirit in your life.

Accepting Christ into my life compelled me to shift my thinking. I was seeking a renewal in my mind, body, and spirit. I recall having shared with a friend that I was undergoing a transformation, and his recommendation to me was to change the people I would hang around with, the places I would go to, and the worldly things I felt brought value to my life before I sought kingdom thinking and living. He also told me that putting anything before God would cause things to fall apart. God must be first in all areas of my life.

Even though I understood all of this, I was still being pulled toward the darkness. I was led into a bookstore, just to see if there was a demand for people inquiring about the satanic bible. At this point my relationship with the Lord was very new. I was a young Christian. New Christians must get into a Bible-teaching church and get mentored by mature believers to support them as they grow in Christ.

I got to the bookstore and found the satanic bible on the shelf. As I reached for the book and attempted to open it, I was overcome by a force that commanded me to close the book and run out of the store. Having done just that, as I proceeded to walk away from the store, I looked down at the crucifix that I was given just after moving from the Bronx. I saw that the body of Jesus had somehow lifted off the cross and was leaning forward, as if it had melted off the cross. It was at that point that the light bulb fully illuminated in my heart and mind. I would live my life for Christ.

TURNING POINT

Do you know how large a mustard seed is? It is very, very small. God says to come to him with the faith of a mustard seed, and he will provide the rest. I have always believed that despite my struggles, somewhere in the middle of my hell I had to have some small mustard-seed amount of faith.

I sit back today and think of the things I have gone through, the things that made me change, and the things that gave me the audacity to believe there was any other power greater than the power of God. I serve a powerful and praiseworthy God. He loves me and has loved me unconditionally. He loved me when I could not love myself. He loves you too.

I liken my story to the story of Job, in that the devil tried his best to get Job to curse God. But despite the devil doing everything in his power except kill him, Job would not curse the name of God. All that Job experienced, God allowed to happen so that in the end the glory would be given right back to God.

We all have experienced our own personal hell on Earth in some way. We have all been tested. If you have not yet been tested, you will be at some point in your life. God allows these experiences to happen to us to make us more reliant on him to glorify him and to develop a closer walk with him. Use your Job experience to ask God what he needs from you and how, even during your time of pain, you lend yourself to be a blessing in the life of someone else or most importantly to the kingdom.

SPARKPLUGS

Consider the following questions. Think of your responses before actually writing down your answers. Be as honest with yourself as you can. Answering these questions for myself was the first step that began the change in my life.

Answering the questions won't be the end. I am charging you to review your progress weekly, and if there are tasks you need to get done, do them. I would lastly recommend that you keep a journal of your progress.

Your thought process and responses to the list of questions will start you on your journey of self-love, acceptance, and change.

- ❖ *Have you ever prayed the prayer of salvation in which you willingly allow Christ to come into your heart? If you have not invited the Lord into your life, please recite the following prayer of salvation and truly believe in your heart the words you speak, and salvation will be yours.*

   The Salvation Prayer

   Lord Jesus, I come into your presence to submit my life into your arms. I wholeheartedly believe you are the Son of God. I thank you for dying on the cross to pay the price for my sins. I confess and repent of my sins. Forgive my sins, and give me the gift of eternal life. I ask you to come into my life and my heart and to be my personal Lord and Savior. Mark me with your blood. Redeem and protect me from Satan and eternal death. Thank you for saving me, Lord. I pray this in the most precious name of Jesus. Amen!

9live's "Finding a Way Out"

❖ *Are you spending time in the presence of God daily?*

❖ *Are you a member of a Bible-teaching church?*

❖ *Do you spend time reading and learning the Word of God?*

❖ *When was the last time you were a blessing to someone?*

Notes:

Chapter 4

Finding Your Way out of Isolation:

A Day in the Life of a Caveman

And the Lord God called to Adam and said to him, "Where are you?"

—Genesis 3:9

Andrew Ross

It was a cold winter night in early 1980, and I was living with my parents. I can remember not having a bed to sleep on and having to put together two big black-velvet-covered chairs, which were located in the living room, to create a place to sleep. I would put those chairs together and imagine I was in a cave. I would cover my head with a blanket and escape into a world of my own.

As I crossed over into my own world, I would begin to picture a very large room with no one else there but me. For that moment, the chairs made me feel as if I had no one to report to, no responsibilities, and no feelings to deal with. I would later make a connection with this makeshift cave to the cave I would create in my isolation from the world. My isolation would develop out of my need to feel safe, my need to actually feel nothing at all. I would use it as an escape from the bullying and the abuse in my home.

The isolation I would create both internally and externally was directly correlated to the behavior my father exposed us to growing up—odd behavior, like never using the front door of the house. He would only use the backdoor. He would enter the home from the back of the house only after using his signature knock, which would alert the family he was home and preparing to enter the house. He would announce himself the same way every time he entered the home. He did this up until he died.

Upon entering the home, he would then put two very large wooden boards in front of the door to deter intruders and even visitors from wanting to enter. He would make his way from the back of the house to the front to seal up the front door with a cloth. This type of paranoid isolation went on for years. I am certain that in my father's mind, he thought he was doing his best to keep us protected from the outside world, but he could not have been further from the truth.

The environment of my childhood home metaphorically was very much like a cave. My home was this dark space where feelings and emotions other than pain and hurt were not welcomed. We were never free to express ourselves because the mood and emotion of my dad determined the atmosphere of the home.

It was my mother who suffered the most from this isolation and abuse. She was constantly being accused of things she had not done. She was frequently accused of having sex with other men and women when my father was out of the home. None of this was true, at least not the part about it happening when he wasn't home.

My parents had a very unique relationship, separate from the abuse. They were swingers. This meant that they welcomed other couples or singles into their sexual experiences. They would get dressed every Saturday night and go to Forty-Second Street to frequent clubs that other swingers attended and to engage in sex all night. My mother reported this to me. They would often engage in very aggressive sexual experiences. I'm not at all certain if this was a lifestyle my mother really enjoyed or if my dad imposed it upon her.

They would walk into the house early Sunday morning fighting, after being out all night. My dad would usually hit my mother in the face, swelling and blackening her eyes. Sometimes, while in my black-velvet cave in the living room, I would hear couples passing through to go to my parents' bedroom, where they would engage in sexual intercourse. Yes, my parents hosted and participated in orgies. This was usually the only time my dad let company in the house.

Living this life firsthand taught me not to feel. I was taught that men don't cry and a woman should be ready to respond to the needs of a man, even at the expense of not caring for herself. My father abused my mother verbally, physically, emotionally, and sexually.

I came to believe that the only way to express myself was through sex and physical contact. I began getting involved with women and lusting after them, not knowing how to feel or how to love. I would put myself out there to get involved with women who were like me: emotionally unavailable or emotionally unstable.

I do recall feeling very conflicted about this because I wanted to be loved. I wanted to be held and cared for, but the act of loving and being loved was foreign to me. This damage prevented me from getting emotionally involved with women for years, simply because I did not know how.

As a result of being emotionally unavailable, my self-doubt and low self-esteem were exacerbated. All my emotions were affected in such a way that I came to abuse myself and use drugs as a way out. The cave I created was my protection from everyone, including myself. I would keep secrets in the cave. I would make myself believe I was doing well. I was coping. But I was wrong. We were not designed to grow or thrive in darkness. God did not create man to be alone.

I did grow to invite people into my world, into my space, after being accused and convicted of a crime. Once you have been officially accused of a crime and booked and are awaiting trial, it seems like the whole world invites itself into your life.

In late 1990, I was getting Chinese takeout in Queens when I got into a staring match with a couple of guys waiting on their food. The rage that consumed me once we exchanged words was indescribable. One of the guys uttered those provoking words of, "What you looking at?" I lost it. I pulled from my pants leg a very large firemen's ax, the kind used to break down doors in a rescue. I began carrying the ax as a means of protecting myself. I had been assaulted, beaten, and almost lost my life at the hands of attackers. I needed my own protection.

Once I pulled the ax out, I cut into this man's flesh. I cut him for every time I was bullied. I cut him for every time my father had beaten me, and I cut him for every other bad thing that had happened to me in my life. I was tired, and he gave me all the reason I needed to go off.

Having hurt another living being to the degree that I hurt that man is something that even now makes me feel remorseful. He did not die, but the injuries he sustained were enough for me to be convicted and sentenced to two and a half years in prison.

While incarcerated, I experienced isolation from a different perspective. I was no longer held down by the abuse of father or the bullies who created a world of terror for me. I was now isolated by a system that sought to hold me back, a system whose sole purpose was to create a savvier criminal rather than supporting the men in jail in developing themselves past the crimes of their convictions.

Jail is a place I have no intention of visiting again in my life. The things I experienced while there were not suitable for a human or an animal to experience. I saw men killed, raped, and beaten up, and I never cared to know the reasons why. I stayed away from drama as much as possible. I just wanted to do my time and get home. The cells were so dark and gloomy, and the infestation of bugs and mice had to be a health hazard. I recall waking up one morning, after having accidentally gotten peanut butter on my t-shirt before falling asleep, to find mice holes in the shirt I still had on my back. The mice had eaten through my shirt while I was asleep.

Despite the violence and the vermin, I was still able to get high, just I did on the street. Like I said, jail is the place criminals go to hone their skills, not to get reformed from them.

While incarcerated, I developed a relationship with a female friend of a good buddy of mine who was locked up with me. We hit it off, and upon my release, she was my lady. However, I still was not ready to handle a relationship full of emotion and feelings. She just filled the void temporarily. Several months later the inevitable happened, and the relationship was over. After my release, this would happen several times. I got involved, only to break things off.

Relationships were damaged; women left me and I left women because we would get tired of the emotional rollercoaster. I got off the emotional ride of doubt, fear, and isolation in 1994. God granted me the most special gift I have ever been given. My daughter was born. I worked very hard at maintaining the relationship I had with the mother of my daughter, but it too became damaged due to the emotional roller coaster we were both on. Despite the failure of the relationship, I was determined to have a connection with my daughter. She would not only know who her father was, but I would remain present in her life.

TURNING POINT

For twenty-one years, I pushed people away. I refused to take responsibility for dealing with the feelings I had toward myself and women. Since my relationship with Christ has developed, I have seen married couples demonstrate that love is real and that relationships can be healthy. These couples daily prove to one another several things: First, when you love Christ first, he will work things out for his glory. Second, you can be married and in a healthy relationship without isolating yourselves. Third, you can decide to stop carrying past baggage around and begin life again.

After all, God has not created anything under the sun that is bad. Sex and relationships are both good, provided the relationships are based on healthy feelings and emotions and the sex is happening within the marital covenant. God created woman to coexist with man.

There is no time like the present to work on all of your unresolved issues and unpack all of your baggage. Holding on to the hurts of the past hurts you and the people you are connected to, and it also grieves the heart of God. The Lord loves us with all he is. He wants the best for us; pain, hurt, and isolation are not on the list of things God wants to see happen in our lives.

We have a personal responsibility to ourselves to let go of the spirit of guilt, the spirit of low self-esteem, the spirit of doubt, and the spirit of isolation, replacing them with the spirit of faith, the spirit of power, the spirit of love, and the spirit of fellowship.

SPARKPLUGS

Consider the following questions. Think of your responses before actually writing down your answers. Be as honest with yourself as you can. Answering these questions for myself was the step that began the change in my life.

Answering the questions won't be the end. I am charging you to review your progress weekly, and if there are tasks you need to get done, do them. I would lastly recommend that you keep a journal of your progress.

Your thought process and responses to the list of questions will start you on your journey of self-love, acceptance, and change.

- *Are you spending time in the presence of God daily?*

- *Do you currently isolate yourself from people? If yes, why are you isolating yourself?*

- *What are the top five issues you need to unpack from your baggage?*

- *Is there anyone in your past you need to forgive for something he or she has done to you? Also consider persons who have passed away when answering this question. Forgiving someone is not an act to be done for the person who hurt you. Forgiveness is given to free you from pain.*

Notes:

Chapter 5

Finding Your Way out of Pain:

Addicted to Pain

For I consider that the sufferings of this present time are not worthy to be compared with the glory which shall be revealed in us.

—Romans 8:18

When I was about twelve years old, my mother and father began having poker parties that would start on Friday night and go though till Sunday night. These parties, along with the orgies, always confused me, because my dad hated for people to be in our home. I guess these two types of events were okay because the focus really was not on the family. The focus was on him feeling like "the man." Whatever his reason, I enjoyed the company because it took the pressure off me for a while.

There would often be major disputes as people got drunk and began losing their money. My mom would have food for the guests, and they played good music. I can remember looking forward to the end of the parties because I would love to go around and clean up, and I would find loose change that I would use to buy candy.

Most of all, I liked to try what was in the glasses that caused everyone to be in such a good mood. It was JB Scotch. This was my parents' favorite drink. It was the drink my dad poured for himself every day after work.

I enjoyed the way the Scotch made me feel. Once I got hooked on the way the drink made me feel, I would sneak a taste when I got in the mood. My dad had a bar in our home, and he kept a fresh bottle of JB for his daily consumption. I believe my dad could have been considered a functional alcoholic because he drank daily. Both of my parents would drink until they got drunk, and then they fought. This impressed upon me that this was normal behavior. As a result, I grew into my adolescence and young-adult years drinking to get drunk, fighting, and getting locked up and not always in that order.

I lived in a neighborhood where most of the guys from the block drank and smoked pot. I was already familiar with drinking because of my home environment, so my introduction to smoking pot was inevitable. My first experience with smoking pot knocked me flat on my butt. I mean, I actually just about passed out. But once I got the hang of how it made me feel, I came to enjoy the altered state. I enjoyed it so much that at the age of fifteen, I smoked pot every single day. The altered state allowed me to forget the pain I was experiencing both inside and outside of the home.

The high gave me a sense of freedom, and it filled the void and gave me a false sense of control. Smoking connected me to the tough guys from the block. This gave me a pass from the bullies picking on me. What I could not see then, with my naïve mindset, was that by getting connected to these guys, the bullies got bigger, and so did my problems.

At sixteen, one of the guys from the block laced the pot with a white substance. I noticed but really did not think to question it because my goal was to remain part of the group. I was cool, I was down, and when the joint was passed to me, I smoked. After a few minutes of inhaling, I felt a completely different high. My mouth got numb, sort of like how you feel after having dental work done. I whispered to one of the guys, "What the hell was that?"

He responded, "You just smoked your first whoola."

"Whoola?" I responded.

"Yes, crack and weed."

I fell in love with this new high, which lasted all of ten minutes, if that long. I chased wanting to feel that first high for the entire time I used drugs. I never found it. I should have been getting ready to graduate from high school, but I became strung out on pot and crack. I was hanging out every day and most of the night, figuring out ways to get more drugs.

My parents turned out to be my biggest support during this time of my life. They would literally lock me in the house. My mom would make sure I rested and ate. They would hold all the money I would earn from working construction jobs with my dad. All of their loving efforts to help me were pointless, because for an addict 5 percent of the problem is the drug and the other 95 percent is the person's attitude and behaviors.

During this time of severe addiction, I was still dealing with an emptiness and void that caused me to feel alone even in the company of other people. My parents lovingly held me hostage for just about three months before I could no longer resist the call of the drugs. I had to get high. I had to be on the street.

The night I left is one I will never forget. My father and I got into a big fight. He expressed his concern for me being an addict, and I denied having a problem. We went back and forth. He wanted me to get help, but I denied needing any kind of intervention, because I did not have a problem. For some reason, in that moment, he opened my dresser drawer, where he found a loaded .45-caliber gun that I kept in the event I had problems on the streets.

In my rage, I shoved past my dad, took the gun and all the money I had saved, and put on a hat that covered my ears (as I recall, it was a very cold winter night). Then I left the house to go on what would turn out to be a four-day binge. I smoked so much crack that night that I ran out of all the money I had left the house with. I then resorted to attempting to use the gun to ensure I could continue to get high.

I began circling the block for two hours. I needed another fix, and robbing someone to achieve my goal of getting high and staying high was my plan. However, no one was on the street. A short time after this, I noticed in the distance some guys walking toward me. As they got closer, I identified them as members of a local gang. They approached me and accused me of robbing one of their friends. Talk about karma! They took guns out and pointed them at my head; at this point, I knew I was going to die. But God...

One of the guys told me to strip down naked; I did as I was told, and I took off my clothes with no hesitation despite the fact that it was very cold outside. I had a choice to do as I was told and strip or get my brains blown out by the six guns pointed at me. When I had all my clothes off, they told me to run home. Since I was about five blocks from home, I began to run. I hopped a fence and immediately began to look for something to put on.

Crazy enough, as I searched for something to put on, I thought about David Banner, the calm alter ego of the Incredible Hulk. I thought of how David would transform back to himself after the Hulk had come out, and he would look in backyards on clotheslines for clothes to put on. On that cold winter night, I was David Banner. However, instead of finding clothes, all I found was a cardboard beer box, which was just enough to cover my private parts. Once I was covered, I ran into traffic to hail someone, anyone, to help me get home.

By the grace of God, I saw a friend who was able to take me home. When I got home, my sister opened the door, and at the first sight of me, she screamed for my dad. My dad rushed from the bedroom, took one look at me, and grabbed his .25-caliber pistol and his camera. The camera was to take a picture for the sake of nostalgia, and the gun was for the guys who had done this to me. My dad had concerns about me bringing my street problems to the house, and he commented that he would kill me the same way Marvin Gaye's father had killed him if I did bring my trouble to his front door.

You would think this eventful winter night would have caused me to change, but it did not. The next day I was back on the street. I sold the sneakers off my feet and the coat off of my back just so I could get high, and the addiction was just getting started.

By the age of nineteen, heroin became my new love. I began selling drugs of all kinds, heroin being my biggest seller. I wanted to be like Tony Montana in the movie *Scarface*. I wanted to be the biggest, baddest dealer in Queens. I was doing okay for a dealer with an addiction. I had big gold jewelry, I had my own apartment, and I had a spot that I was selling my product from. Until I tried heroin. There was a line in the *Scarface* movie, "Never get high on your own supply." I went from making good money to selling everything in my apartment to feed my habit. I stole from my family and friends and robbed strangers.

I was arrested and locked up so many times that most times I could not recall the charge. I was high. While locked up, my body would begin to detox. Sadly enough, my addictions to alcohol, marijuana, pills, cocaine, crack, and sex put me in places that not even an animal would dwell. I wanted to use despite the risk, danger, and pain the addiction was causing me.

There was no detox, rehab, therapeutic community, jail, or institution that could convince me I was an addict. I liked the feeling I got in the dark hallways, underground cellars, and vacant lots. There is an instant gratification one gets from getting high, and I looked forward to that feeling. For the short time the high would last, I felt secure.

When the addiction gets that bad, you justify using to be more social or to celebrate anyone's special day, even if you don't know him or her. In the end, you discover you are using just so you don't wake up sick. You are no longer using to get high; you are using to get straight. There were times when I would physically get sick. I would be in my apartment and begin to have body aches and chills. I would defecate on myself and throw up. The addiction to heroin is really a physical high. Your body actually craves the drug on what seems to be a cellular level.

I had gotten to the point where I would seek to get that immediate security—the rush of the high and the heightened anxiety—any way I could. I was so desperate that I transferred the experience of getting high over to sex. I allowed myself to become addicted to sex in the same way I was addicted to drugs. I would masturbate three times a day. Very similarly to copping drugs, I would rush home to surf the Internet, searching for that feeling and exciting myself to the point of ejaculation. Self-stimulation, as well as with a partner, had become my next chase. I knowingly slept with women who were HIV positive, not being concerned about my health but invested more in the rush of ejaculating. Sex had become as thrilling as getting high. I miraculously am not HIV positive.

TURNING POINT

There is a physical pain an addict experiences as he comes down from or detoxes from being high. The body craves the drug, and this is why stopping is very challenging. The body develops a pattern of dependency on the substance. Replacing the habit of using substances is like replacing any other bad habit for a good habit.

To get rid of a bad habit, you must first be able to replace that old habit with a new healthy habit. Research suggests that it takes about twenty-one days for a new habit to develop. In addition to the replacement of the old bad habit for the new healthy habit, it is essential to get the support of someone you trust to hold you accountable for being successful with your decision to change.

Understanding that change is not an event but a process (Dr. A.R Bernard) must be key in your evolution of change. When you understand this, you will be less likely to become discouraged, as change happens in slow, consistent intervals. Give yourself credit for any and all of your success in the process.

If you are willing to make the investment in yourself and the process, I can assure you that there is light at the end of the tunnel, and the change will happen.

SPARKPLUGS

Consider the following questions, and think of your responses before actually writing down your answers. Be as honest with yourself as you can. Answering these questions for myself was the first step that began the change in my life.

Answering the questions won't be the end. I am charging you to review your progress weekly, and if there are tasks you need to get done, do them. I would lastly recommend that you keep a journal of your progress.

Your thought process and responses to the list of questions will start you on your journey of self-love, acceptance, and change.

- *Are you spending time in the presence of God daily?*

- *What two old habits do you need to change?*

- *What two new healthy habits can you replace the old habits with?*

- *Do you have any addictions you need to deal with?*

- *If yes, do you need support in dealing with the addiction?*

Notes:

Chapter 6

Finding Your Way out of Self-Doubt:

You Are Worth More than You Think

For I know the thoughts that I think toward you, says the Lord, thoughts of peace and not of evil, to give you a future and a hope.

—**Jeremiah 29:11**

I have always been an ambitious person. I can recall hustling at the age of ten. I would sell comic books and custom jewelry, pack bags at the supermarket, and mow lawns. Whatever it took to make a dollar to buy candy, I would do it. I always felt in my heart that I was worth so much more than I was presented with as a young boy. I felt that I was born to be wealthy. But the life circumstances I was born into prevented me from reaching my fullest potential.

School was not my thing growing up. I wanted to make money. I always felt like I was slow. I never seemed to do as well as the other kids. Things just never made too much sense to me, despite the fact that I would attend school every single day before the bullying and the drugs began.

Because of my insecurities about my grades, I never looked forward to report-card day. In fact, I would be thinking of ways to hide my report card from my parents the night before. This plotting never did work, because my sister and I were in the same grade and in the same class, and she looked forward to showing our parents her straight-A grades.

My dad would look at me, then at my report card, and then back at me. He would then proceed to call me a dumb negro. Because of the lack of support at home and in the classroom, I began to believe I had a learning disability and that I was worthless.

9live's "Finding a Way Out"

The feelings of worthlessness began in grade school. Once this thought of worthlessness had fully taken root in my head and in my heart, the drug abuse began. My self-worth was so low that I wanted to die. I would inhale the fumes of spray-paint cans and marijuana together to alter my state of mind. There was no one in my life to support me, to tell me I was worth something or that I could do anything I put my mind to.

No one believed in me, so I did not believe in myself. The drugs helped me to not have to deal with these feelings. I would search high and low for anything to take me away from myself and this life, so as to not feel worthless.

I would get high on drugs and drinking. I would drink so much that I would throw up thick black liquid. By this point in my life, I had decided school was not for me, so I dropped out and began working with my dad. Even while teaching me a trade, my father was verbally abusive. It sounds like an oxymoron, but it was true. I was taught and abused at the same time.

I would get up to go to work each morning, wanting to be home before the day had even gotten started. The pressure of the abuse on the job was painful and stressful. The drugs and alcohol were exhausting, getting verbally and physically abused was exhausting, getting bullied was exhausting, and feeling worthless was the icing on the cake. I wanted out of my life. Who was I kidding? I wanted out of life, period. Killing myself was very attractive to me as a solution to my pain.

During my incarceration, I attempted to complete my high school education. I worked on my general equivalency degree

(GED), but I was still unable to focus. I attempted to take and pass the GED exam three times. The feelings of self-doubt resurfaced again. I was even more convinced that I had a learning disability no one had taken the time to explain to me.

Ironically, while I was locked up, my father was my biggest support system. He and my mom came to see me every time I was eligible for a visit. They sent me packages and wrote letters. I thought it was very interesting that my dad was able to demonstrate his love for me in this way.

I concluded that the mind of an abuser is very similar to the mind of an addict. He gets tunnel vision on what the goal is, be it getting high or beating the life out of the abused. While the act is occurring, the focus in the moment is separated from the feelings of love each would respectfully have for self or the abused. He did love me in a twisted way, just like I loved myself very deep in my soul.

I served two years and came out even crazier and more unbalanced than when I went in. I was so off that I wanted to hurt myself and others. It was at that time in my life that God really showed me just who he is. My daughter was born. She came into this world on October 8, 1994, and changed my life forever.

I became determined to deal with my demons; I was now responsible for this new life, my baby girl. I slowed down my reckless and irresponsible behavior. However, slowing down was not enough, and my demons continued to win. My extremely damaged id and ego would hinder me from being the father I wanted to be to my daughter.

9live's "Finding a Way Out"

For the first time in my battle, I decided to go into a therapeutic drug community. I remained in the community for eighteen months. I was successful in completing all the requirements of the program and graduating. This for me was larger than life, because I had never completed anything in my life. I received a certificate of completion, which made it an even grander accomplishment.

I remained clean and sober for some time after the graduation. I began to deal with many of the feelings that caused me to use in the first place. To help me with the ride of getting past these feelings, I got into a relationship with a very beautiful woman who was also in the program. She was not only beautiful, but she also had been diagnosed with full-blown AIDS.

In this woman, I thought I had found true love. I thought she was the end of my search. We would have long talks about having children together. It had gotten to the point that we would have unprotected sex because I was in love with her. How could I walk away from her? She was honest with me, and her body felt good when I entered her without a condom. We had just reached the two-year mark when I discovered that she had the same issues I had, which were low self-esteem and a mission to end her life.

After realizing that her issues and my issues together were a train wreck waiting to happen, I tried to respectfully end the two-year relationship, but things got crazy. She began to stalk me and leave insane messages on my phone. It had gotten to the point where I had to move and change my number because she would not leave me alone. Don't get me wrong—I was not a victim, and there are two sides to every story. I am certain that to her, I did my dirt and played a role in the outcome of the relationship.

By God's grace, I did not get infected with AIDS. What I did get was a wakeup call. After the breakup, I began to feel more heaviness in my life than usual. The baggage had been overloaded with the possibility of having become HIV positive. I needed to make some changes and make them fast. Up until this point in my life, all of the decisions I had made were based on what other people had told me about myself and what other people were doing. Most importantly, my decisions had been made based on what I had come to believe of myself.

The next chapters of my life were in many ways more challenging than the beginning chapters, as now I would begin to embark on correcting all the wrong, self-defeating, antichrist-like thoughts, feelings, and attitudes that had shaped the first chapters of my life. I had to begin to tell myself and believe that no matter what, my faith was what would carry me and that God does not make mistakes. God created me with a purpose, and I needed to find out what that purpose was.

My new challenge would mean renewing my mind. I had to completely change the people, places, and things I associated with. I had to begin to live from a place of expectation rather than from what I feared would happen. If I expected the best from my life, the best was what I would receive.

We commonly tend to judge our present experiences based on the wreckage of our past. Doing this can prevent people from thinking they deserve the best God has to offer to them. When I was going through my personal hell, I would expect the worst, due to my lifestyle, the people around me, and the environment. The circumstances and the expectation I had attached to my life then would result in the worst taking place.

Today I practice saying what I expect to happen, praying hard, and watching for God to show himself. Things I have accomplished in the past ten years have far exceeded my wildest imagination. However, in the mind of God, he had already had this part of my life established for me to walk into and embrace.

TURNING POINT

To get where I am today in my growth and development, I had to first unpack all of my baggage. All the negative adjectives that I could think of to describe myself—stupid, skinny, dumb, not worthy of love, and so many more—had to be put out of my mind. I had to relearn who Andrew was. I first worked on my relationship with God. Then I found men walking with Christ from whom I could learn and model in my walk as a man, a father, and one day a husband.

I grew to improve my prayer life with God, but more importantly, I now listened to hear from God. I listened to how he could use me to be a blessing in someone's life. Learning about myself also meant being alone with myself to know what I liked and disliked about who I was and to cultivate who I wanted to become.

SPARKPLUGS

Consider the following questions, and think of your responses before actually writing down your answers. Be as honest with yourself as you can. Answering these questions for myself was the first step that began the change in my life.

Answering the questions won't be the end. I am charging you to review your progress weekly, and if there are tasks you need to get done, do them. I would lastly recommend that you keep a journal of your progress.

Your thought process and responses to the list of questions will start you on your journey of self-love, acceptance, and change.

- *Are you spending time in the presence of God daily?*

- *Are you able to spend time with yourself?*

- *Self-esteem rating: On a scale from one to ten, what would you give yourself and why?*

- *How do you show that you love yourself?*

- *What three things would you change about yourself?*

Notes:

Chapter 7

Finding Your Way toward Balanced Temperament:

A Diamond in the Rough

Count it all joy, my brothers, when you meet trials of various kinds. For you know that the testing of your faith produces steadfastness.

—James 1:2–3

Andrew Ross

*G*rowing up, I did not have an effective male role model to look up to. What I did have were male role models who represented extreme control. The balance of love and strength was something I had to teach myself much later on in my life. In my home, my father was always upset or fighting; in my community, men were always angry for one reason or another. All of this energy transferred over to me in that I was a very angry young man. I would go to sleep angry every night and wake up angry. These overtly and subliminally imposed feelings might explain some of the decisions I made in my life, whether wanting to connect to a gang, carrying weapons, and cultivating the self-hate I carried around for years.

There was not a complete balance of love and strength in my dad, but there were rare occasions when I could see balance in him. I unknowingly took in those experiences and used them as a point of reference for the kind of man I wanted to become.

Despite his shortcomings, I did look up to my dad. I wanted for him to love me so badly the way any son would want to be loved by his father—with compassion, support, and empathy.

I watched my dad get up and make an honest day's wage every day. He would leave the house at six o'clock in the morning and return at six o'clock in the evening. In his better moods, when he was not working, my dad would spend a lot of time in the backyard building something or tending to the garden. He grew tomatoes, cucumbers, potatoes, berries, and collard greens.

My most impressionable memory of my father, aside from the abuse, was his amazing work ethic. He would rise very early to accomplish daily work tasks that I often thought he was crazy for doing. But what I did learn was that working for what you want is the only way to obtain it.

He was a tradesman. He knew how to do any and all carpentry work, and he taught me how to paint with precision, sand floors, install plumbing, and lay ceramic tiles. For ten years I worked with my dad, even when I was getting drunk and high. What I did not realize then was that the skill of carpentry trains you to have patience and discipline and to pay attention to detail.

My dad once took on a job that was probably bigger than he could handle at the time. He agreed to rerun plumbing pipes for a building in the Bronx that housed just about one hundred families. Being the proud, strong, and confident leader he was, he gladly took on the job with my help and the assistance of just two other men. The amount of stress that my dad experienced before we completed the job must have been extremely heavy at times. But the alpha male that he was prevented him from breaking his composure in the presence of the man who hired him or the men he had hired.

I share this to demonstrate that there must be a balanced temperament in our lives. The stressors my father took on, coupled with his childhood secrets, affected his ability to demonstrate full balance in our home life. My dad did the best he could, given his lack of awareness and education and his unwillingness to repair some of the trauma he experienced as a young man. Despite his flaws, I learned about the work ethic, true integrity, and discipline from my father.

My mother was equally as strong, simply based on the abuse she endured to keep her family together. By ensuring that her children were raised with the presence of their father in the home, she taught me that love is unconditional. She had mastered using what we had, which was very little, and making everyone feel a sense of family, despite it being tainted by the abuse. My mother was the glue that kept us together. She was the balance of peace to my father's rage. My mother, in my opinion, was a model of what a real woman is.

My mother tried with all she had to love me past my pain. She was there with me in the middle of my personal hell, loving me as only a mother can. She did not pass judgment and knew in her heart that I was better than the decisions I had chosen for myself.

Despite the pain of the abuse, I did have a balance from what each of my parents offered me. What I could not gain from my father, my mother sacrificed to give to her children.

I could not have understood this when I was young because then the pieces that make up my puzzle would have been different. The lens through which I now choose to see the way I was raised has changed due to growth, maturity, and the favor of God. Choosing a lens of being grateful for all things determines your success or failure.

If it is granted by God for you to wake up another day, know that you will experience a trial or a struggle at some point in the day. We are all works in progress. I look at myself today and know who I am and to whom I belong. I have learned through my struggle that despite it all, I am a child of God, and I have been created to have dominion over all. It has become my Christian responsibility to renew my mind daily and have the light of Christ resonate from me in such a way that when I enter a room, without saying a word, the evidence of Christ in my life is felt.

TURNING POINT

My experience has balanced my temperament, and my shift in attitude about the trials in life has allowed me to walk with the spirit of peace. I am a man of God, empowered by Jesus himself to share the good news of the glory of God with the world. I wake each day with the spirit of expectation in my heart, knowing God will demonstrate just who he is and allow me to take part in that miracle.

My journey is not yet over, and my experiences have fostered a reliance on God that I will never walk without or take for granted.

The demons of my past still haunt me. They whisper to me in the addictions that my mother and sister now struggle with and show themselves in the poor decisions my niece and daughter are making with their lives. Despite the demons, I trust that God is all knowing and ever faithful. The pieces of our lives make us, shape us, and prepare us to be just what God needs us to be, in God's time. What I trust is that God is all things to all who trust, remain steadfast, and believe that he is able.

SPARKPLUGS

Consider the following questions, and think of your responses before actually writing down your answers. Be as honest with yourself as you can. Answering these questions for myself was the first step that began the change in my life.

Answering the questions won't be the end. I am charging you to review your progress weekly, and if there are tasks you need to get done, do them. I would lastly recommend that you keep a journal of your progress.

Your thought process and responses to the list of questions will start you on your journey of self-love, acceptance, and change.

- *Are you spending time in the presence of God daily?*

- *Do your words mirror positive outcomes in your life?*

- *Do you wake each day with an attitude of gratitude?*

- *Do you wake up each day expecting God to reveal himself to you?*

- *What changes do you need to make to adjust your attitude?*

Notes:

Chapter 8

Finding Your Way toward Purpose:

A Mission to Live on Purpose

And we know that all things work together for good to those who love God, to those who are called according to his purpose.

—Romans 8:28

Andrew Ross

The word *purpose*, biblically defined, suggests a deliberate plan, a proposition, an advanced goal, an intention, and a design. God has deliberately planned my life and the lives of all believers. Often, it is hard to praise and honor God when you are in the heat of battle with the enemy. At my lowest, most trying times, I would never acknowledge God for his goodness. I would question him as to why he was sitting around not helping me when I was getting high at a young age or when I was incarcerated. My conversation with God would be that my life was his fault. I asked if he was such a good God, why would he allow these tragic things to happen to me?

Having accepted Christ into my life, now I can look back and shout with all my heart that God is good. God knew me before the beginning of time. He made me especially to praise him. I have been fearfully and wonderfully made. However, to gain this reality, I needed to be challenged, in the ways I have been challenged, to shape and develop my character and relationship with God. God is so awesome that he created man to have free will. This free will allows man to make his own decisions, and God's hope is that we will make the decision to love him and ask him into our hearts and that as believers we will choose life.

The amazing thing about God is his mercy. His mercy covers the saved and the unsaved. When I was incapable of making the best decisions for my life, I was still covered by God because he knew that he had a planned purpose for my life. God makes no mistakes despite the mistakes we make. He will use our error for his edification, which is what he has done in my life.

God asks for us to come to him, broken and fragmented, so he can put us together again and make us whole. It is what we choose to do with our pieces that will determine God's effectiveness in creating change in our lives. Yes, God can create the necessary changes in any life in an instant, but he wants us to willingly come to him. The pieces are all the tragedy, the accomplishments, the lost lives, and the birth of children. The events of your life in their totality make up the pieces to our life's puzzle. There are four key issues in my life that have given birth to my understanding and acceptance of my life's purpose.

Pieces (My Experiences) + Puzzle (My Life) = Purpose (God's Plan for My Life)

Puzzle Piece #1: Verbal and Physical Abuse

Purpose: God has turned this piece of my life into the purpose of being able to effectively support individuals who are experiencing this issue, to counsel them out of abusive situations, and to get them to a place of self-love and acceptance.

Puzzle Piece #2: Addiction

Purpose: I am purposed to use this piece of my puzzle to speak to the lives of individuals with addictions and to provide them with solid biblical counsel about freedom from this stronghold.

Puzzle Piece #3: Suicide and Violence, both Self-imposed and Impressed Upon

Purpose: I am purposed to use this experience of my life to help others release the feelings of self-hate and hurt.

Puzzle Piece #4: Depression

Purpose: I am purposed to counsel all who suffer from this strong force to effectively get to a better, more stable sense of self and a balanced existence.

Our life experiences are not random. They are not accidental, and they are purposed. We will often ask ourselves the "what if" questions. What if things had not happened this way, or what if I would have made this decision over that decision?

Despite the decisions we make and the consequences we experience as a result of those decisions, God walks with us. His unconditional love carries us and sustains us, despite our failure and shortcomings.

In Christ we have been given the choice to choose life or death, good or evil. In choosing life, believers must build up a resistance to negative feelings and continue the daily task of renewing their minds to have a Christlike attitude toward the challenges of life.

When I was a young boy, my father would give me the annual task each spring to turn the soil and de-weed the garden in the back of our home. I was not certain why he would request this of me each year, but I did as I was told. One year I got up enough courage to ask him why he asked me to turn the soil. His response was that turning the soil helps the vegetables and fruits develop during the summer months.

We can compare our minds to the garden in that we need to consistently remove the bad thoughts in our minds (de-weed), flip our thoughts (turn the soil), and create new habits (plant new seed) for old habits and fragmented pieces in our lives to be developed into new, healthier thoughts and habits.

TURNING POINT

Self-assessment is one of the most challenging things one can do. However, it is most essential in the development of self. We need to look at the pain, the struggle, and the successes and allow those experiences to aid us in understanding our individual purpose. What makes this process most fascinating is that we all have a unique purpose. We all have been created with special and distinct talents, gifts, and abilities. God expects us to use all of them to the fullest of our potential, to be a blessing to others and to the kingdom.

The issues of low self-worth and self-acceptance, if left unresolved, can hinder one from maximizing his or her full potential. Often, resolving these kinds of issues requires support and counseling, and for the born again, it requires Christian prayer. Anything that can block you from fully developing your purpose is not the will of God for your life.

For the believers, we want to stand before the throne of God on judgment day and be told, "Well done, my good and faithful servant," because we would have done all that we could with our talents, gifts, and abilities.

Use my story and the sparkplug questions to truly begin a conversation with yourself to assess the baggage in your life that needs to be unpacked, so that the real you can begin to live your life on purpose.

We can see the sad consequences of unresolved issues in the news on a daily basis. Hurting people hurt others and themselves. As Kingdom representatives, we are obligated to share the wisdom and good news of the Kingdom with others, so lives can be saved and God's purpose fulfilled in our lives and in the world.

SPARKPLUGS

Consider the following questions, think of your responses before actually writing down your answers. Be as honest with yourself as you can. Answering these questions for myself was the first step that began the change in my life.

Answering the questions won't be the end. I am charging you to weekly review your progress, and if there are tasks you need to get done, do them. I would lastly recommend that you keep a journal of your progress. Your thought process and responses to the list of questions will start you on your journey of self-love, acceptance, and change.

- *Are you spending time in the presence of God daily?*

- *Are you actively seeking God to direct you toward your purpose?*

- *What are your talents, gifts, and abilities? These are the things that you enjoy doing and that come naturally for you.*

- *What steps can you take to develop your talents, gifts, and abilities, once you have identified them?*

- *Are you actively seeking God to turn poor decisions of your past into the successes of your future?*

If you or someone you know is struggling with any of the issues discussed in the book, please log on to www.dreamsofmotivations.com for resources and support.

Be blessed as you begin the journey of finding your way out.

Notes:

Made in the USA
Charleston, SC
01 December 2013